Ont.) British American Commercial College (Toronto

Students' guide for actual business

Ont.) British American Commercial College (Toronto

Students' guide for actual business

ISBN/EAN: 9783741182433

Manufactured in Europe, USA, Canada, Australia, Japa

Cover: Foto ©Andreas Hilbeck / pixelio.de

Manufactured and distributed by brebook publishing software
(www.brebook.com)

Ont.) British American Commercial College (Toronto

Students' guide for actual business

COMMERCIAL COLLEGE

TORONTO.

UDENTS' GUIDE

FOR ACTUAL BUSINESS.

AND 114 KING STREET WEST.

TORONTO:

THE OFFICE OF THE "GLOBE" NEWSPAPER.

1879.

STUDENTS' GUIDE

FOR ACTUAL BUSINESS.

TO THE STUDENTS.

Your promotion to this department is *prima facie* evidence of you ability to apply the principles of Double Entry Book-keeping to a ordinary business transactions.

You have also established yourself in a creditable style of writing o that you are able to enter up the records in the necessary books in usiness-like manner, as well as to execute with creditable skill th arious forms of business paper.

These acquirements are now to be put to the test; and as yo dvance in the exercise before you, you will understand more clearl he kindness of your teachers in holding you to strict account in th latter of style and arrangement.

You are now to exercise your own judgment, and rely upon you wn knowledge, to a greater extent than heretofore. Having passe our apprenticeship, you now emerge into the light and freedom of master-workman. Your tasks will be laid out for you in the rough nd you will receive, from time to time, such hints as will tend to kee ou in the right track. But the details of the labour will be yours ours the honour of success, and the responsibility of failure.

You will now understand that the duties of an accountant ar 1onotonous and laborious, but, at the same time, invested with a pe iliar charm and interest to those having a taste, either natural o: :quired, for positive results and artistic effects.

You have learned the truc value of neatness and order in arrange 1ent, and the importance of looking after small matters, which, taker

The exercises which follow will afford the most ample opportunity for the display of ingenuity and skill, as well as for the application of science. You will be careful to understand and carry out with fidelity the instructions given, as thus only can you hope to realize the benefits which you seek.

You must not for a moment forget that the object and aim of all your operations are to afford you matter for *record*. To this end you should seek variety, and so conduct your business as to necessitate every species of record which can occur in actual business, and especially to introduce documents of every form and character. It is of little consequence whether your business be prosperous or the reverse, so that you are furnished with the material and labour calculated to perfect you in the duties of accountantship.

Above all, be prompt in your dealings with others, that they may not suffer from your negligence. Let every day's business stand by itself, and never put over till to-morrow what should be done to-day. Time with you should be measured, not by *hours*, but by *duties performed*. The habits which you here form will follow you in life, be they good or bad. It therefore behoves you to guard every step, that you may carry with you nothing that will not advance you in the right direction.

The following regulations should be strictly observed :

1. Be promptly on hand at the appointed times for practice and recitation.

2. Deposit all funds in the Bank at the close of each day's business,

3. Keep such record of the maturity of paper as to render it impossible that a note or draft should go to protest by default.

4. In case it becomes necessary to be absent from your classes for a day or more, be sure to arrange your business affairs so as to cause no inconvenience to others or yourself.

5. When shipments are received from other Colleges of the Association, dispose of them *immediately*, and make returns. Always give precedence to foreign correspondents.

6. In the final closing up of a business, present a correct statement of your resources and liabilities to your teacher for further instruction.

The various sets which appear in skeleton here, together with the duties connected with the general offices through which you will pass are intended to afford you sufficient practice to prepare you for the pos

' accountant in any business establishment. Whether these intentions
:e fulfilled will depend wholly upon yourself.

The following is the routine of business :

FIRST SET.

Each student will be furnished with the necessary blanks for
:tual business. He will also be furnished with ($1,000) one thousand
)llars College money, for which he will be required to deposit one
)llar with the principal. Upon closing up his business and return-
ig all his College money, he will receive the one dollar deposited.

Any student who shall buy, sell or give away any College cur-
:ncy shall render himself liable to suspension or expulsion at option
' principal.

The books required are—Day Book, Journal, Ledger, Cash Book,
ill Book, Check Book, Note Book and Pass Book.

The student will fill at least four pages in his Day Book with
)na fide entries, among which will be required the following transac-
ons :

Each purchase and sale to consist of not less than three cards.

Each deposit to be not less than $50 in paper, and 50 cents in
)ecie.

All notes must be placed in Bank for collection.

Each student is required to preserve the invoice of every purchase
ade, all account sales papers, cancelled notes, returned checks, etc.,
id produce them at the end of each set.

In the 3rd and 4th sets Bills Receivable and Bills Payable must
: posted from Bill Book.

Make 12 purchases ; 3 on account, 3 for cash, 3 on notes, and 3
)r which he will accept drafts. He will make 12 sales ; 3 on account,
for cash, 3 on notes, and 3 for which he will draw drafts.

He will receive 2 simple consignments, to be sold on account and
sk of consignor, and will render an account sales when sold. He wil:
:nd 2 shipments to be sold on account and risk of consignor, and wil:
raw on consignee for a portion of the invoice.

If there are stocks in the market he will make as many purchases
nd sales as practicable. He will deposit his Bills Receivable in the
ank for collection. He will draw four checks on the bank, and will at
:ast make five cash deposits. When four pages of his Day Book are
ill he will journalize on loose paper, and have journalizing checked by
ne of the teachers. He will then write it in his Journal, and will pro
:ed to post his books, after which he will balance the Ledger and bring
own balances. His work will then be examined by one of the teachers,
nd if found correct he will proceed to his second set.

SECOND SET.

This set is a continuation of the first. A partner will be admitted who will share in gains and losses in proportion to amount invested Books used same as in first set. The Journal, however, is used differ ently, having three columns instead of two. This set is intended for i small retail business. The student will fill four pages of his Day Bool as before. He will make his purchases in same manner as in first set buying in large quantities and selling in small, and make at least 2(sales of Mdse.

On their maturity he will renew two Bills Payable, paying one hal cash and giving his note for balance and interest. He will make 1: sales ; 2 for cash, 3 for notes, 3 for part cash and part on account, an(4 on account. All sales not settled in full at time of purchase must b written in Day Book in full, showing each item. He will discount ; notes on College Bank, and on their maturity he will renew two of then for the parties for one-half, interest to be included in renewal note He will draw four drafts and accept four, two of which latter he wil renew for the parties as before. He will receive one consignment, t(be sold on joint account and risk of consignor and consignee, each one half, and will render account sales.

He will send one shipment on same terms, and will draw on con signee for a portion of the invoice.

He will deposit all notes remaining on hand in College Bank fo collection. He will, at least, make five cash deposits in College Bank

He will write two letters in connection with his business to partie with whom he is dealing, and will submit them to the principal for ex amination. He will purchase and sell stocks as before, and when hi set is completed he will journalize as before (with the exception o Mdse. Cr., which will be explained to him). When his posting is com pleted he will write out a Balance Sheet, and submit it for examinatioi to one of the teachers. If it be found correct he will proceed to clos his Ledger by a Journal entry, which will be explained to him, and h will then be ready for the

THIRD SET.

This set is adapted for a wholesale trade, three partners. The book used are Day Book, Cash Book, Invoice Book, Sales Book, Journal Ledger, Bill Book, Note Book, Check Book and Bank Book. The firs four are books of original entry.

In this set the student will make 5 purchases for cash in full, 5 o1 account, 5 part cash and part on account, and 5 on notes. He wil make 5 sales for cash in full, 5 on account, 5 part cash and part on ac count, and 5 on notes. He will discount two Bills Receivable at th Bank, which, on maturity, he will renew for the parties, receiving one half cash and taking new note for balance and interest. He will dis count renewal notes at Bank as before.

He will also renew 2 Bills Payable, paying one-half cash and giving ew note for balance and interest. He will obtain one accommodation .ote, which he will discount at Bank, and which he will retire at matuity. He will draw three drafts to his own order, two of which will be ccepted and returned to him, and he will discount them at the Bank, he third he will pay to a private party on account. He will deposit remainder of notes in College Bank for collection. He will receive three onsignments, to be sold on joint account and risk as follows :

1st. Consignor, $\frac{1}{2}$; consignee, $\frac{1}{2}$; and will render account sales.

2nd. Consignor, $\frac{2}{3}$; consignee, $\frac{1}{3}$; will render account sales with orrect average time.

He will at least make seven cash deposits in College Bank.

3rd. Consignor, $\frac{3}{4}$; consignee, $\frac{1}{4}$; will render account sales before be goods are all sold, with correct average time, and will enclose letter o consignor, in relation to matters connected with the consignment. n each case the consignor will draw for a portion of the invoice. He vill send three shipments on same terms as above, and will draw on onsignee for a portion of the invoice.

On the completion of the above transactions the student will jourlalize his Day Book, and will post from Journal, Cash Book, Invoice Book and Sales Book. He will make out Balance Sheet as before and valance the Ledger, bringing down balances as in first set. He will hen submit his work for examination, and proceed to the

FOURTH SET—Four Partners.

This set is same as third—same books—posted into third. The itudent will make 3 sales for cash, 3 on credit and 3 on notes. He will nake 9 purchases on same terms. He will discount 3 Bills Receivable it Bank. He will draw 3 drafts on parties owing him, two of which ie will discount as before. He will renew 3 Bills Payable, paying onehalf cash and giving note for balance and interest. He will receive 3 :onsignments and send 3 shipments on joint account as in last set, and n addition he will receive two consignments as follows :

1st. On joint account and risk of consignor, consignee, and a hird party, each $\frac{1}{3}$, for which he will render account sales, with correct :quated time as before.

2nd. On joint account and risk of consignor, $\frac{2}{3}$; consignee, $\frac{1}{6}$; ind third party, $\frac{1}{6}$; with a certain amount added by consignee,—render iccount sales, etc., as before.

He will at least make ten cash deposits in Bank.

He will send two consignments on same terms, advising third party, ind drawing on him for a portion of his share of the Company, also on :onsignee for a portion of his share. He will purchase and sell stocks, vill write three letters in connection with his business, which must be iubmitted to the principal for examination. He will make out three

accounts current, entering interest, if any, in his Day Book. When his
set is completed he will make out Balance sheet as before. The part
nership will then be dissolved, three of the partners retiring, and bein
paid off in such property as may be agreed upon, or in cash, as the cas
may be. The student will then collect all outstanding debts and pay al
liabilities, and will close all accounts in the Ledger, close the Cash
Book, and wind up the business.

SINGLE ENTRY.

In this set he will make 8 purchases and 15 sales ; 8 of the latte
to be on account, and 3 on notes. He will discount 3 notes at Bank
and renew one of them at maturity. He will send 3 shipments and re
ceive 3 consignments, some of them on joint account. He will drav
and accept 3 drafts.

He will post his Ledger by figures, and on closing will have 12 ac
counts, from which balances are to be brought down. He will find los
or gain, and will change from Single to Double Entry, and will continu
to set for two pages of the Day Book, when he will journalize, post an
close up as in former sets.

SIX COLUMN JOURNAL.

Books used are Six Column Journal and Ledger.

Adapted to a Retail Trade.

The student will make two (2) purchases on account, two (2) fo
cash, and two (2) on notes. He will then make nine (9) sales on account
writing down all the items, two (2) for cash and two (2) on notes. H
will draw three (3) drafts and accept three (3); discount three (3) Bill
Receivable at Bank, and will renew two (2) of them for part. He wil
renew two (2) Bills Payable, receive two (2) consignments and two (2
Mdse. Companies, and send two (2) shipments and two (2) Shipmen
Companies. He will post his "Sundries" columns daily, and at the en
of every three pages will post the footings of all the other columns
Posting will be done in each case by figures. He will, on the comple
tion of above transactions, proceed to close his Ledger as usual, and wi
submit his work for examination.

COMMISSION.

Books used are : Commission Sales' Journal, Commission Journa
and Ledger, together, with the remainder of the auxiliary books, Cas
Book, Bill Book, etc., etc. The student will receive 15 consignment
as follows :

Two simple consignments on account and risk of Consignor; 4 Mds
Companies on account and risk of consignor and consignee ; 4 Mds
Companies on account and risk of consignor, consignee and third part
each ⅓, in two of which an account sales will be rendered before th
whole is sold.

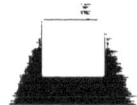

7

Two on account and risk same as last, and the consignee adding a rtain amount.

Three Adventures in Company with three or more partners, to be ld as may be agreed upon with respect to gains and losses. He will cept drafts, discount and renew notes receivable and payable, render account sales for each consignment, make out 3 accounts current, and nd 3 letters in connection with his business. In short, it is expected at in filling up this set the student will diversify his transactions as uch as possible, that he will seek to make a general application of the inciples of book-keeping to all possible forms of transactions. This t will be to some extent considered as a test of the student's abilities a book-keeper, and it is hoped that he will spare no pains to finish it a satisfactory manner. Before closing he will collect all his accounts, id pay off all his liabilities, and will then close up his Ledger in the dinary manner.

He will then proceed to the set designated

MANUFACTURING,

he Day Book of which he will copy into his own. He will fill out ime Book, and will then proceed to journalize and post, after which will make out Balance Sheet and close his Ledger as in former sets. e will then go through

FOREIGN EXCHANGE.

This set shows the method of keeping accounts between merchants ho reside in different countries, especially between those of America id Great Britain. Books used—Day Book, Journal, Ledger, Bill and ash Books; Journal and Ledger are ruled with pound, shilling and ince, and dollar and cent columns; reducing pounds, shillings and pence dollars and cents, and *vice versa*— buying Bills of Exchange on ondon; parties' accounts kept in the currency of their respective untries.

ADMINISTRATOR'S SET.

This set represents the personal estate of a farmer who had leased is farm on shares previous to his decease, and was to allow a reason-le sum for any improvements made upon the farm. The student is ppointed Administrator, and takes possession of the personal effects; converts all the personal property into cash, pays the widow of ceased $100, and divides the balance equally among the heirs, six in umber, for which he takes receipts; he makes out all accounts current, c., notes, drafts, etc., and submits them to the teacher.

STEAMBOATING.

It embraces *eight* different books, viz.: Hands' Register, Hands' edger, Freight, Fuel and Cash Book, Journal and Ledger, all of which

are to record the business of steamers ; besides Pocket Memorandu
Books for taking down Freight as delivered to the Boat, Deck Passeng
Book, Cabin Register, Receipt Book, etc.

BANKING.

At some time during the course the student will enter the Bar
as an officer thereof, and will have charge at different times of all tl
books used therein.

The number of entries of each kind in each set will be required fro
each student, and none will be allowed to leave any set until it is cor
plete and has been examined and passed by one of the teachers of tl
College.

All Balance Sheets must be free from blots, erasures and mistake
and none will be passed in which there is a wrong figure.

He will prepare advertisements of Mdse. which he has for sale, ar
display them on the bulletin prepared for the purpose.

All damaged Merchandise will be destroyed as laid down in tl
College Rules.

THE

STUDENT'S GUIDE

THROUGH THE

ACTUAL BUSINESS DEPARTMENT

OF

ONTARIO COMMERCIAL COLLEGE,

BELLEVILLE, ONTARIO.

W. B. ROBINSON,　　　-　　　-　·　_ ⎫
J. W. JOHNSON,　-　　-　　　·　_ ⎬ PRINCIPALS.
　　　　　　　　　　　　　　　　　　　⎭

mmmmmmmmmmm

"Labor Omnia Vincit."

mmmmmmmmm

BELLEVILLE :

PRINTED AT THE "DAILY INTELLIGENCER" OFFICE, MARKET SQUARE.

1882.

TO THE STUDENT.

—o—

☞Read all instructions carefully before commencing work.

You are now about to carry into practice the knowledge obtained in that portion of the course already completed.

It is supposed that you now possess the qualifications necessary for the proper prosecution of your business, therefore you are furnished with nothing but a "Guide" to direct you what transactions to perform, and thrown upon your own resources.

Your record thus far, shows that you have won for yourself *promotion* through perseverance and honest endeavor; your continuance in the path of well-doing is asked, so that when you have completed the work assigned in this department and pass your final examinations, you will merit and receive the testimonial awarded to all *Good* and *Faithful Students.*

If you find difficulties to contend with, do not become discouraged, or grow faint-hearted, but grapple with them, firmly resolved to surmount every opposing obstacle, and with perseverance you must succeed. The great difference between men, between the feeble and the powerful, the great and the insignificant, is *energy—invincible determination*—a purpose once fixed, then death or victory.

Your previous training has qualified you to execute your work in a neat, business-like style, therefore this will be exacted of you. Do nothing without system. Method furnishes the key to all true progress. Order and neatness should constitute your talisman. "A place for everything and everything in its place," should be your motto and your rule. Blots and erasures in your books will stand as so many accusing spirits, charging you with slovenliness and want of care; while errors and omissions in your record from this forward, cannot be excused but will be marked against you. Let your constant aim be to secure an easy, elegant hand-writing. This is essential to every acceptable accountant, and when once acquired is of itself a valuable capital at starting out on the great highway of life and bespeaks for its possessor characteristic ability, and also gives evidence of other cardinal qualifications, viz.: carefulness, method and exactness. If you are not already a good penman devote every spare moment of your time to practise until you have accomplished your object.

As you are soon to go out into the business world, let it be impressed upon your mind, and ever keep before you this fact:— "The three great requisites of honor and wealth are, *Honesty, Industry,* and *Perseverance.*

GENERAL DIRECTIONS.

———o———

Business Papers must be made out *correctly* and neatly, and be properly stamped and endorsed, when stamping and endorsing are required. Neglect of this will necessitate their being copied.

Invoices and Account Sales will be pasted into the Invoice Book, and all other papers neatly filed.

Examine carefully all papers made for you by others, and refuse any that are not correctly and neatly made out, fit for examination. Should any dispute arise, refer quietly to one of the Principals for settlement.

When buying goods, *always* receive an Invoice and check it carefully in the manner taught in the Business Paper Class. In this connection your attention is again directed to the method of marking the cost and retail price on goods as illustrated in the "Accountant," and exemplified on the cards representing goods.

Promptness and strict attention to business are characteristic of the model business man, these, with neatness and accuracy in your work, are required from every student.

No man can keep books in a hurry, nor make two or three entries at once. Do not try it, a mixed and muddled state of your accounts is sure to follow hurried book-keeping.

Every transaction in the "Guide" *must* be done, unless circumstances make it impossible, but you must obtain the supervising Principal's sanction before passing on. You will often require to do other transactions than those mentioned. In these you will have an opportunity to exhibit tact and enterprise.

Each set will be presented for examination when it is completed. *If not up to the standard you will require to work it again.*

You will require to settle all accounts, bank and others, and discharge every liability before closing your work. Then hand back your currency and receive from the supervising Principal a certificate which you will put in with the last set for examination.

Meet all your notes and acceptances promptly on the day of maturity, and save the dishonor and cost of a protest. Keep a fair balance at your credit in Bank, but should you, on any day, overdraw your account, cover the overdraft before the hour of closing the Bank.

The commission to be charged on consignments is 5%. The rate of interest charged at the Bank for discounting, either accommodation paper or that of your customers, having your endorsation, is 7%, and you are required to work all interest calculations yourself.

When a cash discount is allowed on purchases the amount will be 2½%.

The Bank's charge for making collections is ¼ of 1%, and at the same rate of exchange you can purchase Drafts at the Bank for remitting to a distance.

In addition to keeping an account in your Ledger with the Bank, keep track of your balance on the back of the stubs of your cheque book.

When drawing cheques always make out the stub first, as it serves as an original entry. When you transfer the entry to the Journal or Cash Book put the folio on the stub in large red ink figures, as [J 81]

Get every deposit, discount and collection at the Bank entered to your credit in your Bank Pass-Book, and have the book balanced at the end of each set and receive back your cheques and any notes and drafts that may have been charged, giving the Bank a receipt for them, on the printed form.

You are to take the utmost care of the Bank Currency and the Cards representing goods. Loss or destruction of these you will have to make good.

Notes and Drafts are to be made payable at the College Bank.

When entering a draft or note in Journal or Cash Book never omit in your explanation B. R No.. or B. P. No.., as the case may be. In many cases the explanation required will be no more than this ; the numbers refer to the Bill Book, where the full particulars of every bill are recorded.

6

SET I.

The books used in this set are, Six Col. Journal, Bill Book and Ledger. In this set paste the Invoices into the Invoice Book, (ask to be shown how) and journalize immediately, also for reference put the Journal folio on the Invoice in red ink. Give full explanations under every journal entry, as this is the book of original entry, and be sure to enter the items when you sell on account. You know the consequence to a business man who sues for an account and has neglected this.

——o——

TRANSACTIONS.

1. Draw a Lease of the premises you have rented after the form of "Short Lease not under Seal" (page 209 of Accountant), and have it executed in presence of a witness.

2. Make the opening memorandum of commencing business, stating the kind of business, from whom you have rented the store, the rent you are to pay, and the amount and nature of capital invested. Write an advertisement.

3. Journal entry for investment

4. Memorandum of having engaged ———as book-keeper at $40.00 and (name one other) as clerk, at $30.00 a month.

5. Pay one month's rent in advance and receive a receipt for it.

6. Make a deposit in the Bank.

7. Draw two cheques—one for $6.00 to the order of ——— for one ton of coal, the other for $5.00 to the order of ——— for advertising business.

8. Draw up an accommodation note, at 3 months for $·· and get it discounted at the Bank, and receive net proceeds in cash.

9. Order by letter from Jones & Brown a stock of goods amounting to about $200. (In selling and buying and making shipments confine operations to three or four kinds of goods.) Get a cash dis. of 2½% off, and pay for the goods by cheque.

10. Buy on account, goods amounting to about $50
from an American firm.   Pay Duty $3.00 and
Freight $2.50.

11. Sell on account goods amounting to about. $60

12. Sell for Note at 3 months (all notes to be negotiable
by endorsement) goods amounting to about. . $70

13. Buy goods amounting to about.............. ..... $100
and accept a draft for the amount that will
allow you 13 days for payment after date of
acceptance.

14. Sell for cash merchandise amounting to about... $75

(Memo.—Balance your cash frequently.)

15. Buy a Bank Draft to remit creditor from whom No.
10 was bought, deducting 2½% cash discount.
The Bank's charge for exchange or commission will be ¼%.

16. Buy, giving your note at 3 months, goods amounting
to about............ .... $100
and pay freight on them, $2 by cheque.

17. Ship to a commission merchant, *(make all Shipments
and Shipment Co's at the same price the goods
cost you,)* paying freight $1, for sale on your
account, goods amounting to about.. .... $70
and make out, and get signed, 3 B. Ls., (1 set.)

*(Memo.—Don't put prices in B. Ls. only marks and num-
bers,* (thus, J·W·J·B· No. 130) *on the margin, and description and
weight in body.)*

18. Suppose that some of the goods bought (No. 16)
are not according to order, return those not
suitable (say one card) and receive a Credit
note in acknowledgment.

19. Sell on account goods amounting to about.. ..... $100

20. Buy on account goods amounting to about........ $100

21. Buy for cheque goods amounting to about....... $75

*(Memo.—Make deposits, and discount customers' paper
when you deem it necessary, and pay and receive payments
of notes and acceptances as the business requires, withcut
reference to the Guide. Also make settlements of accounts either
for or against as required.)*

8

22. Receive payment for No. 11 by cheque and allow a discount of 1%.

23. Buy for note @ 3 months, (negotiable by endorsement,) goods amounting to about $50

24. Sell, and get the person to accept a draft that will allow 6 days for payment after acceptance, goods amounting to. $150

25. Receive a consignment of goods to be sold by you on commission, about............ ...... $100 and pay freight on it $2.00.

(NOTE.—Keep consignments and Merchandise Co's. separate from your own goods, and each by itself, and as far as possible make shipments to and receive consignments from other students.)

26. Pay one of your clerks $5 on account.

27. Sell consignment (No. 25) for cash.

28. Render an account sales of consignment (No. 25), charge 5% commission and $1 for storage, and enter the proceeds to the credit of the consignor.

29. Buy on account goods amounting to about $75

30. Sell on account goods amounting to about $100

31. If you have not done so discount a note or acceptance held against a customer.

32. Render statements of account to any customers whose accounts are unsettled, and receive from your creditors statements of account.

33. Pass to the credit of your employees salary earned. Post your Ledger. Leave your Pass Book at the Bank to be balanced. You may leave any notes or acceptances at the Bank for collection. endorsing them to make them negotiable. You will make no entry until the collections have been made and you are notified. Simply put a pencil memo opposite each in the Bill Book. When your Ledger is posted test whether it is in balance. Next take an Inventory of goods, then a Balance Sheet, and finally close the representative accounts into loss and gain, loss and gain into the proprietor's account, balance the real accounts and bring down the balances, checking them with the Resource and Liability Columns of the Balance Sheet. Put the work in for examination.

SET II.

The books required in this set are, Cash Book, Journal Day Book, (in which you will rule a special column for mdse. sales,) Ledger, Bill Book, and Invoice Book. You will paste the invoices into the Invoice Book, as before, but defer journalizing them till the end of the set. You will carry the amount of each invoice (except those for cash or cheque purchases, which will be posted from the C. B.,) into the margin on the right, stating opposite, either term of credit, or, if settled by note or draft, give full particulars, and carry additions of the book forward from page to page.

You will continue the Produce and Commission business, with the resources and liabilities of Set I, as shown on the Balance Sheet, and balances brought down in Ledger.

---o---

TRANSACTIONS.

1. Admit into the business a partner who is to invest $500, and make an additional investment of $500 yourself. Each partner is to receive interest upon his investment at the rate of 7% per annum, after which Gains and Losses are to be shared equally. (See "Canadian Accountant", page 80, for an illustration of this.) Make out Articles of Co-partnership, embodying all the facts relating to the partnership, also state the facts briefly in the Journal.

2. Buy a store, No. 129 Front Street, for $1,500, for which give Cash $500 ; your note at 3 months, with interest at 7%, for $500 ; and a mortgage for one year for $500 at 7%.

3. Pay one of your employees $5 on account.

4. Receive account sales of No. 17 (in last set) and cash for net proceeds.

5. Make a joint shipment of goods, paying freight.

6. Raise $100 by discounting an accommodation note, at 3 months.

7. Buy goods on account amounting to about $100, and pay $2.30 freight.

8. Pay a year's premium to the Canadian Insurance Company upon an insurance policy on store and contents, to the amount of $1,000, at 7/8 of 1%.

9. The following items of expense paid in cash :—Postage $1.30, Stationery, Books, &c., $2.70.

10. Sell for ½ cash and ½ note at three months, goods to the amount of about $120.

11. Renew for 1 month half the amount of a note outstanding against you and pay cash for half.

12. Sell for note goods amounting to about $75.

13. Sell on account goods amounting to about $50.

14. Buy on account goods amounting to about $120.

15. Receive a Merchandise Co. paying $2 freight.

16. Receive a consignment on sole account.

17. Dismiss a clerk, credit him with salary to date and pay him off.

18. Renew ½ of a note for 1 month for a customer, receiving cash for balance.

19. Add to Merchandise Co., (No. 15) goods from your own stock amounting to about $50, and notify the other party.

20. Buy goods on account amounting to about $200, and pay freight $1.50.

21. Sell for cash goods amounting to about $75.

22. Sell goods to the amount of about $75, and get the party to accept your draft that will be due 6 days after acceptance.

23. Buy goods amounting to about $100, and accept a draft at ten days date for them.

24. Sell for cash goods amounting to about $100.

25. Pay the Book-Keeper $15 on account.

26. Buy goods amounting to about $75, and give in payment your check. (Getting it certified at the Bank.)

27. Sell the goods belonging to Merchandise Co A for cash. After you do this render account sales, make the account sales entry, passing the net proceeds to the credit of the shipper.

28. Remit by Bank Draft the amount due on Merchandise Co. A, for which give check.

29. Sell goods to the amount of about $75, and draw at sight.

30. Place in the Bank for collection any notes or acceptances you hold. (Refer to instructions at end of last set regarding this.)

31. Render and receive statements of account, and if desired make settlements either by cash or note.

32. Credit employees with salary and partners with interest, and also credit any sums owing for expenses or the like which have not been settled or credited hitherto.

33. Journalize the Invoices, or post them directly from the I. B.

34 Finally, post your Ledger; leave your pass-book at the Bank to be balanced. When your Ledger is posted test whether it is in balance. Next take an inventory of goods, and inventory Real Estate at an advance of 25%, then take off a Balance Sheet, and finally close the representative accounts into Loss and Gain, Loss and Gain into the proprietor's accounts, and the real accounts into balance, as a new set of accounts will be opened for Set III. Put your work in for examination.

SET III.

The books required in Set III are, Journal Day Book, Cash Book, Invoice Book, Sales Book, Bill Book, and Ledger.

You will open a new set of accounts by journalizing the Resources and Liabilities of the previously existing partnership, as shown in the Balance Sheet of the former business, in one of the two ways mentioned in " The Accountant," at pages 180 and 181.

(Note.—Remember what has been impressed upon you in the class, that to open a new set of books by double entry, either for a previously existing partnership or business, from a badly kept set of double entry books, or from single entry, you must have a statement of Resources and Liabilities, and the proportion of capital belonging to each partner.)

TRANSACTIONS.

1. Admit into the business a new partner who will invest $400 cash.

2. Draw at sight for ½ the Invoice of Shipment Co. (No. 5 transaction in Set 2.)

3. Buy on account goods to the amount of about $50.

4. Buy for 3 months note goods to the amount of about $25.

5. Sell on account goods amounting to about $60.

6. Buy on account goods amounting to about $40.

7. Receive account sales and remittance for shipment Co. (No. 5 transaction in last set.)

8. Buy goods amounting to about $50, and give in payment cheque for ½ and cash for ½.

9. Assume the consignment (No. 16 in Set II) at 10% advance, and after journalizing the transaction make the account sales entry, charging 5% com, and $1 for storage, and remit the net proceeds to the consignor.

10. Make a joint shipment.

11. Sell goods on account amounting to about $20.

12. Receive a Merchandise Co.

13. Draw out for your personal use $25.

14. Sell goods amounting to about $40 and get a draft accepted that will allow four days for payment after acceptance.

15. Renew a note for a customer.

16. Buy goods amounting to about $50, and accept a draft that will be due 3 days after acceptance.

17. Assume the Merchandise Co., (No. 12 Set 3,) after making the entry render account sales and make the account sales entry, charging 2 % Com. and $2 storage.

18. Remit by Bank Draft the amount due the consignor of above Merchandise Co. (this, remember, includes not only the net proceeds but half the invoice placed to his credit when goods were received.)

19. Sell goods on account amounting to about $50.

20. Make a partial payment on a note.

21. Discount one or more customer's notes, have the proceeds placed to your credit in Bank, and entered in your pass book.

22. Receive account sales of Shipment Co. (No. 10 in this set) and net proceeds in cash.

23. Sell goods amounting to about $40, for cash.

24. Sell goods amounting to about $50, and receive a three days date draft on a third party.

25. Buy goods amounting to about $15, for cash.

26. Place in the Bank for collection all notes and acceptances, and render and receive statements of account.

27. Credit employees with salary, partners with interest, and any other debts owing, that are not yet in the books.

28. Journalize the I. B. and S. B. (or post directly from them,) then post the Ledger. Take off a trial balance. Leave your pass book in bank to be balanced. Next make an inventory of goods unsold. Take off a balance sheet, close the representative or working accounts into loss and gain, loss and gain into the Proprietors' accounts and bring down the balances of resource and liability accounts. Finally proceed to wind the business up, as you did the 4th month of the 11th set by converting resources into cash and paying off liabilities, including the partners' capital. Put your books in for examination, and return your currency and get a certificate.

AUDITING.

To audit is to thoroughly examine and report upon the work of an accountant. The value of an audit rests solely upon the competence, honesty, and independence of the individuals who make it.

If they are not thorough accountants it is unreasonable to expect that they will be able to detect accidentally or wilfully false entries, or form an intelligent opinion of the work they have undertaken ; hence a report under such circumstances is the very opposite of the security desired, and which an audit by competent men would afford to a company or corporation.

That auditors should be men of established character for probity it is unnecessary to point out, and that the reliance to be placed upon the work they perform is largely reckoned by their independence, and their being uninfluenced by interested parties, is equally plain. We argue, therefore, that Companies or Corporations are equally bound to employ competent accountants who possess the moral qualites indicated, as auditors, as they are to employ only such to keep their books.

Auditors for Joint Stock Companies are appointed by the Shareholders at the annual general meeting. The reason why the Shareholders, and not the Directors, should make the appointments is very plain. The Officers of the Company are largely controlled by the Directors and the audit being, so far as this connection goes, an examination of the faithfulness to the Shareholders of both the Officers and Directors, it is necessary that the Shareholders themselves should appoint the Auditors.

The Auditors upon being duly appointed should at once begin their duties, as a long delayed audit is far less effective than a prompt one, particularly if only one audit takes place in the year.

The proper manner of conducting an audit is to begin at the books of original entry, at the same time using the auxiliary books and examining vouchers.

The Cash Book might be gone through for the first month and compared with the vouchers; then the Day Book and Journal entries for the same time should be compared, those of the Day Book being verified (as well as those in the Cash Book) from vouchers, documents, auxiliary books, drafts, notes, etc., etc., and proceed in this way from month to month with the books of original entry, checking each transaction thus $\sqrt{}$, and as the work progresses making such memoranda, on which to base the report, as may be deemed proper. Next the Ledger entries should be compared and carefully checked with the books from which they are brought and all additions verified ; the Trial Balance should be then examined and after that the Stock Ledger, the Transfer Book, the stubs in the Instalment Scrip, and Stock Certificate Books, and any other auxiliary books or forms not already gone through in connection with the Cash Book and Journal. Finally a balance sheet showing the Company's Losses and Gains, and its Assets and Liabilities should be made out, and a report in a somewhat similar form to the example should be prepared, for submission to the Directors.

The manner of auditing the books of a municipality or public institution will be on the principle stated above relating to the books of Joint Stock Companies.

EXAMPLE OF AUDITOR'S REPORT.

TO THE BOARD OF DIRECTORS OF THE BELLEVILLE GAS COMPANY —

GENTLEMEN,—I have made a thorough audit of the Books of the Company for the year ending 27th January, 1881, and beg to report that I have found everything correct.

The statements herewith presented are true abstracts from the Books, and accurately represent the operations for the past year, and the present condition of the Company's affairs. I may add that the Books are well kept by a thoroughly efficient system.

J. W. JOHNSON,
Belleville, February 24, 1881.   *Auditor.*

EXAMINATION PROBLEMS.

——o——

A variety of arithmetical problems are here appended, among which are some examination papers given to former graduates. You should work them all over carefully, and thoroughly understand them, before attempting to pass your final examination in arithmetic, as they will give you an idea of the nature of the questions you may expect in connection with that examination.

. 1.   A broker bought stock at 20% above par, and sold it at 20% below par : what per cent of the cost did he lose ? *Ans. 33⅓ per cent.*

2.   Bought a cask of wine containing 42 gallons, at $2.50 per gallon, and 12 gallons have leaked out : at what price per gallon must I sell the remainder, to gain four per cent on the first cost ? *Ans. $3.64.*

3.   Bought 100 barrels of flour at $8.10 per barrel, and sold 90 barrels for what the whole cost. If I sell the remaining 10 barrels at the same price, what will be my total gain and my gain per cent ? *Ans. $90 ; 11⅑ per cent.*

4.   A merchant sold a piece of goods which he had marked 25 per cent. above cost, at 20 per cent. discount from his marked price, thinking he should still make a profit. Did he gain or lose ? *Ans. neither.*

16

5. A grocer sold raisins which cost him $4 per box, at $3.50 per box : how much was the loss per cent ?   *Ans. 12½.*

6. Sold flour at $9 per barrel, which was ten per cent less than the original cost. What would have been the gain per cent, if it had been sold at $10.50 ?   *Ans. 5 per cent.*

7. A gentleman sold two house-lots at $1200 each. On one he gained 20 per cent, and on the other he lost 20 per cent. Did he gain or lose by the transaction, and how much ?   *Ans. lost $100.*

8. A speculator bought 200 shares of railroad stock, at $96 per share. He sold 100 shares of the same at a gain of 5 per cent., and the other 100 shares at a loss of 5 per cent. Did he gain or lose by the operation, and how much.   *Ans. neither.*

9. What per cent. advance on the cost of goods must I ask in order to deduct 10 per cent. from the asking price, and still make a profit of 10 per cent?   *Ans. 22²₉.*

10. A merchant purchased cloth at $3.50 per yard, less 5 per cent. for cash. What was the net cost per yard, and what per cent. must be added to the invoice price, to give a profit of ten per cent ?   *Ans. $3.32½, 4 ½.*

11. A firm, having failed in business, owes to A $1975, to B $4250, to C $1682, and to D $1140. Their assets, less expenses of settlement, amount to $2379.45. What per cent. of their indebtedness can he paid? What dividend will each creditor receive?   *Ans. A $523.37 ; B $1126.25 : 26½ per cent.*

12. I bought a lot of coffee at 12 cents per pound. Allowing that the coffee will fall short 5 per cent. in weighing it out, and that 10 per cent. of the sales will be in bad debts, for how much per pound must I sell it to make a clear gain of 14 per cent. on the cost ?   *Ans. 16 cents.*

13. What must be the asking price of raisins costing $7.364 per box, that I may fall 10 per cent. of it and still gain 10 per cent. on the cost, allowing 10 per cent. of sales to be bad debts ?   *Ans. $10.*

14. I bought a horse of Mr. A for 15 per cent. less than it cost him, and sold it for 30 per cent. more than I paid for it. I gained $15 in the transaction. How much did the horse cost Mr. A? How much did it cost me? For what did I sell it ?   *Ans to last $65.*

15. By selling Java coffee at 18 cents per pound I make a profit of 20 per cent., for how much must I sell it to make a profit of $16\frac{2}{3}$ per cent ?   *Ans. 17½ cents.*

16. The cost of purchasing and transporting a quantity of goods from Montreal to Manitoba is 9 per cent. of the first cost of the goods. If a merchant in Manitoba wishes to make a profit of 25 per cent. on the full cost of the goods, what per cent. gain on the *first cost* must he ask for them? What amount of goods must he purchase in Montreal to realize a profit of $3625 on the *first cost* ? What would be the real profit on full cost?   *Ans. to the last $2725.*

17. What must be the asking price of cloth costing $3.29 per yard, that I may deduct 12½ per cent. from it, and still gain 12½ per cent on the cost ?   *Ans. $4.23.*

18. A wool merchant in Belleville remitted to his correspondent in Montreal the proceeds of a consignment amounting to $2453.75, per draft, which he purchased at the expense of the consignor, at 1½ per cent. premium : what was the amount of the remittance, his commission being 2½ per cent. ?   *Ans. $2357.05.*

19. Received and sold for John Smith, Montreal, 15 sacks of wool. The gross proceeds were $1433.78, and the charges were as follows : Freight, $104.03 ; Drayage, $1.50 ; Wharfage, ⅛ per cent. ; and my Commission 5 per cent. on the sales : what were the net proceeds ?   *Ans. $1254.78*

20. A has a hog weighing 300 pounds, and B has another weighing 500 pounds. C buys both hogs, weighed together, for 5 cents per pound. The three men agree that A's hog, is worth ½ cent more per pound than B's, and shall be paid for at that rate : how much per pound will A and B each receive for his hog ?   *Ans. A, $5\frac{5}{16}$ cts.*
    B, $4\frac{13}{16}$ cts.

21. A merchant ships $31360 worth of wheat from Hamilton to Montreal. For what must he get it insured at 2 per cent. so as to *cover* both the value of the wheat and the premium paid for its insurance ?   *Ans. $32000.*

Explanation.—Since the policy is to cover both the value of the wheat and the premium, and, since the premium is 2 per cent., or $\frac{2}{100}$ of the amount covered by the policy, the value of the wheat must be $\frac{98}{100}$ (or 98 per cent.) of the sum insured. $31360 is $\frac{98}{100}$ (98 per cent.) of what ?

22. For what must a cargo of R. R. iron worth $115200 be insured to cover both the value of the iron and premium, the rate of insurance being 4 per cent? *Ans. $120000.*

23. A merchant shipped a cargo of flour worth $47880 from London, Ont., to Montreal via Belleville. To insure it from London to Toronto, he paid 1½ per cent.; from Toronto to Belleville ¼ per cent.; from Belleville to Montreal 3¼ per cent. For what sum must it be insured to cover value of flour and premium for the voyage? *Ans. $50400.*

24. A policy covering property and premium is taken for $1204½.84. What is the value of the property insured, the rate being ⅜ per cent? *Ans. $12000.*

25. A merchant insures a cargo of goods for $81841.44, covering both the value of the goods and the premium. What is the value of the goods, the rate of insurance being 2 ¼ per cent.? *Ans. $80000.*

26. My agent at Montreal writes that he has purchased for me 4000 bushels of wheat at 80 cents per bushel, and wishes me to send him a cheque on Quebec which he can sell to a broker at a premium of ¾ per cent. How large a cheque shall I send him, his commission being 3 per cent. *Ans. $3271.46.*

27. Foster and Barber sell for S. G. Beatty & Co. 3500 lbs. of butter at 20 cents a lb., 2580 lbs. of cheese at 9 cents per lb., at a commission of 5 per cent. They invest the balance in dry goods, after deducting their commission of 2½ per cent. for puchasing. How many dollars worth of goods do Beatty & Co receive? What is the entire commission of Foster & Barber? *Ans. to last $68.21.*

28. I received of Brown & Lincoln $560 in uncurrent money to purchase books. I pay a broker 3½ per cent. for current funds, and invest the balance after deducting my commission of 2 per cent. What do I pay for books, and what is my commission? *Ans. to last $10.596.*

29. A broker bought 5 shares of R. R. stock at 35 per cent. discount, what is the brokerage at 5 per cent. the par value of each share being $100? *Ans. $25.*

30. An insurance company insured a block of buildings for $350,000 at ⅜ per cent. but thinking the risk too great, they reinsured $150,000 at ¾ per cent. in another company, and $100,000 of it at

⅜ per cent. in another. How much premium did the company receive? How much did it pay to both the other companies? How much did it clear? What per cent. of premium did it really receive on the part not *reinsured*.   *Ans. to last. ⁷₂₀ per cent,*

Note.—All property in one block, or in adjacent buildings, having communications, or on one vessel, is considered as *one risk*, and Insurance Companies seldom take more than $10000 in one risk. Some companies of very large capital take $20000, but small companies do not take more than from $3000 to $5000 in one risk.

31. For what sum must a ship valued at $23470 be insured so as, in case of its destruction, to recover both the value of the vessel and the premium of 2¼ per cent.?   *Ans, $24010.23.*

32. I send to my agent in Manchester $17460 and instruct him to deduct his commission at 3⅛ per cent., and invest the balance in broadcloths at $2.95 per yard. When I receive the goods I have to pay in addition $1347.90 for carriage, $479.40 for insurance, $169.83 for storage, wharfage and harbor dues, and an *ad valorem* duty at 2½ per cent. on the invoice of goods. Required, how many yards of cloth my agent ships to me, and what I gain or lose per cent. on the whole transaction if I sell the goods for $25000.
Ans. 5739.29 yds. ; gain 25¾ per cent.

33. Bought goods of Foster & Barber, at sundry times, and different terms of credit, as follows :

Dec.	18, 1874, a bill of $375.50, on 6 months credit.				
Jan.	10, 1875,	"	290.60, on 6	"	"
March	13,	"	"	800.00, on 8	"	"
April	30,	"	"	650.80, on 7	"	"
June	15,	"	"	460.25, on 4	"	"

What is the equated time for the payment of the whole?
Ans. Oct. 8, 1875.

34. S. G. Beatty & Co. sold goods to J. B. Ashley, at sundry times, and on different terms of credit, as follows :

Sept.	30, 1874, a bill of $ 80.75, on 4 months' credit.				
Nov.	3,	"	"	150.00, on 5	"	"
Jan.	1, 1875	"	30.80, on 6	"	"
March	10,	"	"	40.50, on 5	"	"
April	25,	"	"	60.30, on 4	"	"

How much will balance the account June 2, 1875?
Ans. $364.04.

Note.--The equated time for the payment of the above account is May 5, 1875 hence the several bills above are equivalent to a bill of $362.35 due May 5. It is evident that the $362.35 should draw interest* from May 5, to June 2, the time of settlement. When it is required to know the amount due at any date *previous* to the equated time, the *present worth* of the sum of the several bills must be found.

35. A merchant sold to one of his customers several bills of goods, as follows :

May   9, 1874 a bill of $340 on 4 months' credit.
June   6,   "   "   400 on 3   "   "
July   8,   "   "   345 on 5   "   "
Aug   30,   "   "   130 on 5   "   "
Sept. 30,   "   "   240 on 6   "   "

How much money will balance the account Jan. 1, 1875?
Ans. $1466.40.

36. J. D. Kelly bought of George Ritchie & Co. several bills of goods, as follows :

March   3, 1875, a bill of $250, on 3 months' credit.
April 15,   "   "   180, on 4   "   "
June   20,   "   "   325, on 3   "   "
Aug.   10,   "   "   80, on 3   "   "
Sept.   1,   "   "   100, on 4   "   "

What is the equated time of payment, and how much money would balance the account July 1, 1875?   Ans. Aug. 30 ; $925.65

37. Purchased goods of a merchant at sundry times and on different terms of credit, as follows :

Nov.   9, 1874, a bill of $ 20.00, on 5 months' credit.
Nov.   30,   "   "   50.60, on 3   "   "
Dec.   31,   "   "   90.00, on 4   "   "
Feb.   1, 1875,   "   120.00. on 3   "   "

What is the average date of *purchase*, and what the average time of *maturity?*   Ans. to first Jan. 4, 1875.

38. A merchant sold goods to one of his customers as stated below :

*Six per cent is charged when no rate of interest is specified.

April   6, 1875, a bill of $450, on 4 months' credit.
May   12,   "   "   600,   "   "
June   20,   "   "   750,   "   "
Aug.   1,   "   "   300,   "   "

When must a note for the whole be made payable?

Note.—When the sales have the *same* term of credit, as in the above example, it is most convenient to find *first the average date of purchase.* The equated time of payment is then readily found by adding the common term of credit to this average date of purchase. The average date of purchase in the above example is 54 days from April 6, which is May 30 ; the equated time of payment is 4 months from May 30, which is Sept. 30.

The days of grace generally allowed may be added to the equated time.

39.   Sold W. B. Robinson, on a credit of 90 days, the following bills of goods :

          Jan.   10, 1875, a bill of $20.
          April 12,   "   "   45.
          May   27,   "   "   60.
          June   30.   "   "   75.

What is the equated time of payment?   *Ans.* Aug 14.

                         BELLEVILLE, May 20th, 1874.

$1650.

40.   On demand, I promise to pay to the order of F. A. King Sixteen Hundred and Fifty Dollars, with interest at 7 per cent., for value received.

                             J. A. RAPHAEL.

Indorsements.—Sept. 1, 1874, $25 ; Oct. 14, 1874, $150 ; March 20, 1875, $45 ; July 5, 1875, $300.

What was the amount due Nov. 11, 1875?

Solution.—Interest on $1650 from May 20, 1874, to Sept. 1, 1874, 3 mons. 12 days., at 7 per cent. per annum. -   -   - $ 32.725
The payment, $25, being less than the interest then due, neglecting the former work, find the interest on $1650 from May 20, 1874, to Oct. 14, 1874, 4 mons. 24 dys., -   -   -   -   -   46.20
                                                 1650.

Amount due Oct. 14, 1874, -   -   -   -   -   1696.20
Sum of the two payments, $25 and $150, to be deducted -   -   175.

Balance due after the second payment,   -   -   1521.20

Interest on $1521.20 from Oct. 14, 1874, to March 20, 1875, $46.14, being more than the payment made, find the interest on $1521.20 from Oct. 14, 1874, to July 5, 1875, 8 mos., 21 dys.,   77.201.

	1598.401
Sum of the payments, $45 and $300	345.

Balance due July 5, 1875,	1253.401
Interest on $1253.401 from July 5, 1875, to Nov. 11, 1875, 4 mos., 6 dys.,	30.708

Balance due on settlement, Nov. 11, 1875,	1284.109

Note.—Frequently an estimate of the interest may be made *mentally* with sufficient accuracy to decide whether it be not more than the payment, whereby some labor may be saved.

41.   A note of $1200 is dated June 10, 1871, on which,

Aug,	16, 1872, there was paid	.	$100
Dec.	28, 1872, " " "	.	200
June	2, 1873, " " "	.	25
Dec.	29, 1873, " " "	.	25
June	1, 1874, " " "	.	25
Oct.	28, 1874, " " "	.	500

What is the amount due Dec. 10, 1874, the interest being 6 per cent?
Ans. $551.347.

($1000)   BELLEVILLE, April 10, 1869.

42.   One year after date, I promise to pay to the order of James Johnson one thousand dollars, with interest at seven per cent., for value received.

                                     I. B. SMITH.

On this note were the following endorsements:

Nov. 10, 1870, rec'd $ 80.50.   Jan. 10, 1872, rec'd $450.80.
July 5, 1871, " 100.00.   Oct. 1, 1874, " 500.00.
What remained due Jan. 1, 1875?   *Ans. $170.146.*

14.   MONTREAL, July 15th, 1870.
$650.

     Two years after date I promise to pay to the order of Peter Finn, six hundred and fifty dollars, with interest at 10 per cent., payable annually, for value received.

                                  W. S. WARREN.

Mr. Warren on the above note, Sept. 15, 1872, $105 ; May 9, 1873, $250. What amount was due Sept. 24, 1874?

Note.—In cases like the last, the payments should be applied first to the discharge of the interest *on the annual interest,* then the *annual interest,* and finally the principal. Tne interest on the principal which has not yet become *annual interest,* not being due, should not be cancelled by payments except it be at the final settlement of the note.

Solution.

First annual interest,............	$65.
Interest on the same from July 15, 1871, to Sept. 15, 1872,..	7.583
Second annual interest,.....	65.
Interest on same from July 15, 1872, to Sept. 15, 1872,... ..	1.083
	$138.666
First payment, ...	105.
	33.666
Interest on $33.666 from Sept. 15, 1872, to May 9, 1873,. ..	2.188
Original principal, ...	650.
	685.854
Second payment,...	250
New principal,.....	$435.854
Interest on $650 from July 15, 1872, to May 9, 1873,........	
not due at time of payment, ...$53.083	
Interest on $435.854 from May 9, to July 15,.........7.990	
Third annual interest,.....	61.073
Interest on same from July 15, 1873, to Sept. 24, 1874, ...	7.278
Fourth annual interest,..........	43.585
Interest on same from July 15, 1874, to Sept. 24, 1874, ...	.835
Fifth annual interest, due at settlement,....	8.354
Amount due Sept. 24, 1874, ...	$556.979

43. In a certain adventure A put in $12,000 for 4 months, then adding $8,000, he continued the whole 2 months longer ; B put in $25,000, and after 3 months took out $10,000, and continued the rest for 3 months longer ; C put in $35,coo for 2 months, then withdrawing ? of his stock, continued the remainder for 4 months longer ; they gained $15,000 ; what was the share of each ?
Ans. A. $3,492.06 ; B. $4,761.91 ; C. $6,746.03.

44. Five merchants were in partnership for four years ; the first put in $60, then, 5 months after, $800, and at length $1,500, 4 months before the end of the partnership ; the second put in at first $600, and 6 months after, $1,800 ; the third put in $400, and every six months after he added $500 ; the fourth did not contribute till 8 months after the commencement of the partnership ; he then put in

$900, and repeated this sum every six months; the fifth put in no capital, but kept the accounts, for which the others agreed to pay him $1.25 a day. What was each one's share of the gain, which was $20,000?

Ans. $2,019.65; $4,871.80; $4.815.81; $6,467.74; $1825.

45. On the 1st of January, the firm of Bowers & Murphy was insolvent; and on closing their books, the debit balance against Bowers was $1,437.35, and the debit balance against Murphy, $927,-45. They admit two partners, Thomas Wilson, who invests $4,000 and Henry Brown, who invests $5,000; and continue the business, agreeing that the gains and losses shall be divided as follows :—Bowers is to receive or sustain ⅜; Murphy ⅜; and Wilson and Brown are to share the remainder in proportion to their average investments. At the end of a year their total resources were $22,543.75, and their total liabilities $7,946.45. Bowers and Murphy had each drawn out, as per agreement, $1,200, for personal expenses. Thomas Wilson drew out as follows :—April 1, $300; July 1, $500; Oct. 1, $700. Henry Brown drew out, April 1, $250; July 1, $430; Oct. 1, $600; what was the debit balance against, or credit balance in favor of each partner at the end of the year?

Ans. Bower's dr., bal. $110.33; Murphy's cr. bal., $399.57; Wilson's cr. bal. $6,280.47; Brown's cr. bal. $8,027.59.

46. A, B and C hire 10 acres of pasture for $140, in which A grazes 60 head of cattle for 20 days; B, 20 head for 40 days; and C. 30 head for 30 days. What proportion of the rent should each pay? *Ans.* A, $57.93; B, $38.62; C, $43,45.

47. A and B enter into partnership in business, Jan. 1, 1874, under an agreement that the gains and losses shall be shared equally; but that each shall be allowed interest at 6 per cent., on his capital invested, and be charged with interest, at the same rate, on all sums withdrawn. A invested, Jan. 1, $10,000, and March 1 withdrew $3,000. B invested, Jan. 1, $5,000, and April 1, $5,000 more; and withdrew, July 1, $4,000. On taking an inventory of stock, and closing their books, Jan. 1, 1875, their Total Resources were found to be $29,148 75, and their Total Liabilities, $12,246.25. What did each one gain by interest, and what was his whole gain and net capital at closing? *Ans.* A gained by interest $450; B $405; A's whole gain, $1,973.75; B's $1,928.75.

In the following example the time is reckoned by months, as is usual in business, and the gain is computed by percentage.

48. John Jackson, Hiram Dickerson, and William Wilson, entered into partnership, and invested and drew out as follows;

| John Jackson invested, | July.........1, 1874......... | $1.000 |
| " " " | November...1, 1874......... | 1,500 |

" " drew out,	April........1, 1875.........	300
Hiram Dickerson invested,	July.........1, 1874.........	2,500
" " "	January....1, 1875.......	600
" " "	June.........1, 1875.........	1,000

| Willliam Wilson invested, | July......... 1, 1874 .... | 3,000 |

| " " drew out, | November .1, 1874...,.... | 2,000 |
| " " " | March 1, 1875......... | 500 |

Their whole gain was $15,140, and each partner shares in proportion to his amount of capital invested, and for the time it was employed. What does each partner withdraw July 1st, 1875?

Solution.

John Jackson invested, July 1, 1874, ...$1,000 × 12 = $12,000
                        Nov. 1, 1874,..........:...... 1,500 × 8 = 12,000
                                                                    ⎯⎯⎯⎯⎯
                                                                    24,000
Drew out, April 1, 1875,.... .... 300 × 3 = 900
                                                     ⎯⎯⎯⎯⎯
Capital for 1 month,......... ...... $23,100
Hiram Dickerson invested, July 1, 1874,......... 2,500 × 12 = 30,000
                          Jan. 1, 1875, ... 600 × 6 = 3,600
                          June 1, 1875,......... 1,000 × 1 = 1,000
                                                             ⎯⎯⎯⎯⎯
Capital for 1 month,................ . $34,600
William Wilson invested, July 1, 1874, ... 3,000 × 12 = 36,000
Drew out, Nov. 1, 1874,....... 2,000 × 8 = 16,000
          Mar. 1875,....... ... 500 × 4 = 2,000   18,000
                                          ⎯⎯⎯⎯⎯
Capital for 1 month,........ .... $18,000
                                                            ⎯⎯⎯⎯⎯
Whole average capital for 1 month, ... $75,700
$15,140 ÷ 75,700 = . 20 per cent of gain on the capital for 1 month.

Gain.
Jackson's average investment,....: ....$23,100 × 20 = $4,620
Dickerson's " " ... . 34,600 × 20 = 6,920
Wilson's " " ....···· .... 18,000 × 20 = 3,600
                                                               ⎯⎯⎯⎯⎯
Whole gain (proof)............. .. .. $15,140
Jackson's balance of capital is...... :........... 2,200
  " share of profit 4,620
                                                              ⎯⎯⎯⎯⎯
  " net capital ....,,.......... 6,820
Dickerson's balance of capital is................................... 4,100
  " share of profit........ 6,920
                                                              ⎯⎯⎯⎯⎯
  " net capital. 11,020
Wilson's balance of capital is.................................. 500
  " share of profit......... 3,600
                                                              ⎯⎯⎯⎯⎯
  " net capital.... 4,100

49. A and B are partners. A invested ⅜ and B ⅔ of the capital. They are to share equally in gains or losses. At the close of business the resources are : Cash $6,800, Bills Receivable $4,700, Merchandise $6,400, Real Estate $5,000, Bank Stock $900, Steamboat Stock $9,000 A has drawn from the business $2,365, B has drawn $526. The liabilities are : Firm's Notes unredeemed $4,680, Bal favor of S. S. Packard $620, J. T. Balkins $476, R. H. Hoadley $326. The net gain during business has been $2,644. What was the firm worth at commencing? What was each partner worth?

Ans. Firm $24,945. A $9,978. B $14, 967.

50. C, D and E are partners. C invested ⅛, D ⅜, and E ⅜, to share the gain or losses equally. At the close of business the resources are found to be : Wheat on hand valued at $2,600, Corn on hand $3,200, Flour $1,600, Mill and Fixtures $8,000. The firm owe Digby V. Bell $2,600, to J. H. Goldsmith $1,500, and on their notes unredeemed $949. The net loss in the business has been $633. What was the net capital of the firm at commencing? What was each partner's net capital?

Ans. Firm $10,984. C $1,373. D $4,119. E $5,492.

51. There are four partners engaged in business as a firm, F. G, H, and I. They have been unfortunate, the net loss being $15,-320. On examination the resources are found to be as follows, viz. : Live cattle on hand valued at $9,680, Packed Beef valued at $12,-600, Empty Barrels on hand valued at $500, Deposit in Drovers Bank $2,500. The firm owe on their Notes and Acceptances $22,-600, Warren P. Spencer on account $4,000, J. C. Bryant on account $6,000. The partners invested in equal amounts and are to share the gains or losses in the same proportion What was the investment of the firm? What was each partner's investment?

Ans.—Firm $8,000 ; F $2,000 ; G $2,000 ; H $2,000 ; I $2,000.

To find what extension should be granted to the balance of a debt. partial payments having been made before the debt was due.

52. A owes B $1200, due in 6 months, but to accommodate him paid $400 in 2 months. When ought the balance to be paid?

Ans. in 8 months.

Explanation.—Since A paid B $400 four months *before* it was due, B, at the close of the 6 months, owed A the interest of $1 for 400 × 4 months = 1600 months. To balance this interest due A, he can keep the $800 unpaid ¹⁄₈₀₀ of 1600 months = 2 months after the debt is due.

53. Jones & Brown sold Wm. Wills, June 10, 1874, goods to the amount of $1300, on 6 months credit. Aug. 20, Mr. Wills paid $200 ; Sept. 18, $250 ; Oct. 30, $350. When, in equity, ought the balance to be paid ?

Operation.

days

$$200 \times 112 = 22400$$
$$250 \times 83 = 20750$$
$$350 \times 41 = 14350$$

$$\$800 \qquad 57500$$
$$57500 \div 500 = 115$$

The balance ought to be paid 115 days from Dec. 10, 1874, which is April 4, 1875.

Rule.—Multiply each payment by the time it was paid before due, and divide the sum of the products by the balance unpaid.

54. A sold B, July 1, 1874 goods to the amount of $1500, on a credit of 90 days. Aug. 5, B paid $400 ; Sept. 3, $600 ; Sept. 15, $300. When ought B to pay the balance ?
Ans. April 26, 1875.

55. A merchant sells a customer to the amount of $600, ½ of which is to be paid in 3 months, ⅓ in 4 months, and the balance in 7 months. The customer pays ½ down. How long may he keep, in equity, the remainder ? *Ans.* 8 months.

56. A owes B $600 payable in 6 months. At the close of 3 months he wishes to make a payment so as to extend the time of the balance to one year. How great a payment must B make ?
Ans. $400

Explnaation.—B wishes to pay such a sum of money three months before it is due, as will extend another sum 6 months after it is due. It is evident the sum paid must be twice as great as the sum extended. Divide $600 into two parts, which shall be to each other as 2 to 1.

57. A owes B $1000, payable in 6 months. At the close of 2 months A pays B $1200, and B gives A his note for the balance. When ought the note to be dated ? *Ans.* 24 months back

Explanation.—Since B paid A $1200 four months before the $1000 was due, A, at the close of the 6 months, owes B the interest of $1200 for 4 months, or $1 for 4800 months. It is evident that a note for the balance, $1200—$1000=$200 must be dated one-two-hundredths of 4800 months, or 24 months previous to the time the $1000 was due.

58. July 10, 1875, A paid B $600; Sept. 12, 1875, B paid A $800. When ought A to pay the balance?

Explanation.—Sept 12, B owes A $600 × its interest for 64 days. He paid A $600 + $200. Hence, A is entitled to the use of the balance ($200) until its interest equals the interest of $600 for 64 days, or 192 days. 192 days from Sept. 12, 1875, is March 23, 1876.

59. July 10, 1875, A paid B $800; Sept. 12, 1875. B paid A $600. What should be the date of a note for the balance?

60. A and B are partners. A is to share ⅜ of the gain or loss, and B ⅗. At the close of business the following is shown to be the condition of their affairs, viz: Cash on hand $2680. Bills receivable on hand $3620. Five shares Montreal Bank Stock valued at $520. House and lot valued at $6000. Sturgis & Co. owe on account $1800. The firm owe on notes outstanding $2840 They owe G. P. Carey on account $890. A invested $4610. B invested $4860.

What is A's interest in the concern? *Ans.* A $5178
" B's " " " B $5712

Note.—In the following example the resources are supposed to be brought in at their actual cash value. No interest is allowed on the partners' accounts unless so specified.

61. C, D and E are partners. To share the gains or losses each one third. The resources and liabilities at the close of the year are found to be as follows, viz: Money deposited in Bank $8460. Mining stock valued at $10240. Bills receivable on hand $6420. Bank Stock on hand valued at $3826. Block of buildings and Lot valued at $35000. Hall & Co., owe on account $1344. L. M. How owes on account $960. The firm owe on their notes unredeemed $5680. To Mason & Co., on account $1700. C invested $18420. D invested $18460. E invested $18432. What is each partner's present interest in the concern!
Ans. C $19606, D $19646, E $19618.

62. F, G, H, and I are partners. They share the gains or losses as follows, viz.: F and G ¼ each, H ⅓ and I ⅙. At the close of business the resources are cash $4628, Merchandise $12620. Real Estate, $5000, Bank Stock $3000, Wheat and Corn $2800, Horses and Harness $500, Lumber $520, Money deposited in Merchants Bank $8620. F has drawn from the business $450, H has drawn $180. The liabilities of the concern are, Notes unredeemed $4600, due Simon & Co. on account $800, due S. S. Jones on account $1200. F invested $6682. G invested $6682. H invested $8908. I invested $4454. What is each partner's interest in the concern? *Ans.* F, $7480; G, $7930; H, $10392; I, $5286.

63. J, K, L, M, and N are partners. The gain or loss is to be divided as follows : J $\frac{5}{15}$, K $\frac{4}{15}$, L $\frac{3}{15}$, M $\frac{2}{15}$, N $\frac{1}{15}$. Upon examination the following is found to be the condition of affairs at the close of business, viz : Notes on hand against other parties $12680, R. R. Stocks $8420, Town Debentures, $6000, Bank Stock $2800, Bonds and Mortgages $9460, Deposit in Bank $6742, R. C. Bank owes the firm $4286, Brown and Bros. owe $1520, Interest on Notes, and Bonds and Mortgages in the hands of the firm $688. Office Furniture on hand valued at $824. The liabilities of the concern are as follows, viz : Notes and Acceptances outstanding $5486, Interest due on firm's Notes and Acceptances $280, Bal. favor Trader's Bank $2626, Bal. favor of Merchants Bank $1500, N invested $2287, M invested $4575, K invested $9150. L invested $6861, J invested $11455. What has been the Net Gain? What is J's interest in the concern ? K's ? L's ? M's ? N's ?

EXAMINATION PAPERS.

——o——

EXAMINATION NO 1

——o——

Fifteen questions are given in the Final Examination on Arithmetic, and each student is required to work. at least, twelve of them correctly in order to pass the examination.

The following are Examination Papers formerly used which will serve as an example of the problems you may expect.

1. Find the interest on $574.80 for 1 year 7 months and 27 days at 8 per cent. per annum. *Ans.* $76.2568.

2. What sum must I put on the face of a note, payable in 90 days, so that I may obtain $425 when discounted at the Bank at 7 per cent. ? *Ans.* $432.826.

3. What must be the asking price of raisins costing $7.364 per box, that I may fall 10 per cent. of it and still gain 10 per cent. on the cost, allowing 10 per cent. of sales to be in bad debts? *Ans.* $10.

4. My retail price for broadcloth is $4.75 per yard, by which I make a profit of 33⅓ per cent. I sell a wholesale customer 100 yards at a discount of 30 per cent. from the retail price. What per cent. do I gain or lose, and what do I receive per yard?

Ans. 6⅔ yer cent. ; $3.32½ per yard.

5. A merchant failing owes A $800, B $500, and C $1000. His property is valued at $1850. What will each Cr. receive?

Ans. A $643.470; B $402.18; C $804.35.

6 Remitted my Agent in N.Y. $1000 in gold with instructions to deduct his com. at 2 per cent. and invest the remainder in flour then selling at $7.50 per barrel U. S. currency. How many barrels of flour should I receive; gold being quoted $1.20. *Ans.* 156 ⁶⁴⁷⁄₇₅₀.

7. I have received from my correspondent in London £275 sterling with instructions to deduct my commission at 3 per cent. and invest the balance in Canadian Tweeds, worth $1.20 per yard. How many yds should I send him? *Ans.* 1082 ¹⁹⁄₂₄.

8. For what sum must I insure a cargo valued at $2000, so that in case the whole is lost I may recover both the value of the property and the premium of 3 per cent.? *Ans.* $2061.8554.

9. Two persons A and B enter into copartnership agreeing to share gains and losses according to capital invested. A put in $2500 and B $1200 ; after they were in business 7 months A withdrew $1000 and B invested $500 more, at the end of the year they have gained $3150. How should it be divided?

Ans. A $1879.474; B $1270.525.

10. What is the Compound Interest on $1000 for 4 years at 5 per cent. per annum? *Ans.* $215.506.

11. A vessel in her passage from Quebec to Liverpool, became stranded, when it was found necessary to throw overboard 1500 barrels of flour, worth $7.80 per barrel, belonging to J. S. Miller. The contributory interests of the vessel were as follows : Holton & Co. had on board Mdse. $9500. Ritchie & Co had on board Mdse. $6500 N Jones had on board Mdse. $10,000. The value of the Vessel was $45000. Net Freight $7000. Amount paid another vessel for assistance $900. Seamen's wages and board $450. Expenses of supplying new rigging $1500. How much should J. S. Miller, receive for the flour thrown overboard?

Ans. $9867.40

12. J Collins in account with W. Ponton.

Dr.					Cr.			
Jan.	1, to Mdse. $1000 on 3 months credit.				Jan. 30 Cash $ 800			
Mar. 20,	"	2000 on 4	"	"	Feb. 1	"	1000	
May 1,	"	500 on 3	"	"	April 1	"	200	

When should a note be dated to balance above account ?

Ans. Dec. 23

13. There are two bins the one 4ft. 6 in. long, 4ft. wide, and 3 ft. 6 in. deep, and the other 5ft. 4 in. long, 4 ft. wide, and 3 ft. 6 in. deep. How many bushels will be left after filling these bins from a pile on the floor in the shape of a cone 12 ft. in diameter and 8 ft. high? *Ans.* 128 bush.

14. What is the capacity of a circular cistern 9 ft. deep, and 7 ft. in diameter. How many barrels will it hold ?

Ans. 68.7.

15. What is the storage on flour at 3 cents per barrel per month received and delivered as follows :

Received.				Delivered.			
Jan.	1,..	.. 400 bushels,		Jan.	30,..	.. 800 bushels.	
Jan.	24...	.. 600	"	March	4,..	..1100	"
Feb.	8,..	..1000	"	June	6,..	.. 300	"
Feb.	20,..	.. 400	"	July	1...	.. 40	"
May	4,..	.. 50	"				

What is the amount of the above bill rendered Sept. 1st, and how many barrels of flour on hand ? *Ans.* $118.52 am't. of bill.

———o———

EXAMINATION, NO. 2.

1. Find the interest on $784.50 for 2 yrs. 11 mo. 19 dys. at 7 per cent. per annum. *Ans.* $163.067.

2. What sum must I put on the face of a note, in order that I may receive $340.50 when discounted at a bank, at 7 per cent. per annum. The note being drawn for 3 mos.?

Ans. $346.77.

3. What is the compound interest on $256, for 3 years at 6 per cent., payable annually? , *Ans.* $48.899.

4. $116.67. BELLEVILLE, May 1st 1865.

On demand I promise to pay John Smith, or bearer, one hundred and sixteen dollars and sixty-seven cents with interest, for value received.

On this note were the following endorsements :

Dec. 25, 1865, rec'd. $16.66   July 10, 1866, rec'd. $ 1.67
Sep. 1, 1867, " 5.00   June 14, 1868, " 33.33
Apr. 15, 1869, " 62.00

What was due Aug. 3rd, 1870?   *Ans.* $23.789.

5. Three graziers A, B, and C, hold a piece of ground in common, for which. they are to pay $75 a year. A, on the 1st of Jan. puts in 12 sheep, on the 1st of March, 8 more, and on the 1st of June takes out 10. B, on the 1st of Jan. puts in 15; on the first of Feb. takes out 6, and on the 1st of July puts in 12 more. C, on the 1st of Feb. puts in 14, on the 1st of April 4, and on the 1st of August takes out 9. How much of the rent ought each to pay at the end of the year?
   Ans. A, $23.814 ; B, $28.762 ; C, $22.422.

6. Received from my correspondent, London, £264, 16s., 10d. sterling, with instructions to deduct my commission at 3 per cent., and invest the balance in Canadian Tweed, worth $1.25 per yard. How many yards should I send him?   *Ans.* 1,001.15 yds.

7. Remitted my agent in N. Y., $2,340 in gold, instructing him to deduct his commission at 2 per cent., and invest the balance in Flour worth $7 per barrel, U. S. Currency. How many barrels should I receive? Gold worth $1.10.
   Ans. 360.504 barrels.

8. I bought a quantity of Tea at $1 per lb   Allowing that the tea will fall short 10 per cent. in weighing it out, and that 15 per cent. of the sales will be in bad debts, for how much per lb. must I sell it to make a clear gain of 20 per cent. on cost?
   Ans. $1.568.

9. If I own a vessel valued at $7,493, and I wish to insure it at a premium of 4¾ per cent. so as to recover, in case of the destruction of the vessel, both the premium paid and the value of the vessel, for what sum must I insure?   *Ans.* $7 854.29.

10. A merchant asked for a quantity of goods 30 per cent. more than they cost him, but becoming damaged he was obliged to sell them at 12 per cent less than his asking price. He gained $150 by the transaction. What was his asking price, and for what did he sell them? *Ans.* $1354.166, asking; $1191.666, selling price.

11. What is the storage on wheat at 3 cents per bushel per month, received and delivered as follows:

Received.			Delivered.		
Jan.	1,	900 bushels.	Jan.	28,	2500 bushels.
Jan.	9,	1200 "	Jan.	31,	400 "
Jan.	14,	800 "	Feb.	27,	6000 "
Feb.	8,	1500 "	Mar.	8,	1500 "
Feb.	12,	1000 "			
Feb.	26,	4000 .'			
Mar.	1,	2000 "			

Account rendered June 1. *Ans.* $210.50.

12. Sold Flour on commission at 4 per cent. and invested the net proceeds less my commission at 3 per cent. in salt. My whole commission was $250. What was the value of the flour and the salt? *Ans.* $3,678.57 flour; $3,428.57 salt.

13. M. Grass in account with E. Roy.

Dr.				Cr.			
Jan.	1, to Mdse.	$	800.	May	1, by cash	$	850.
Jan.	28, "		2000.	May	29, "		1000.
Feb	1, "		1000.	Aug.	1, "		1500.

Account rendered Oct. 1, 1871. When does the balance average due? *Ans.* Jan 7, 1868.

14. A steamer in her passage from Quebec to Liverpool became stranded when it was found necessary to throw overboard goods belonging to Turner & Co., to the amount of $1000. The contributory interests were as follows:—Value of vessel $55000; J. Smith & Co. Mdse. $4000; Hamden & Co. Mdse. $3000: Turner & Co. Mdse. $2000; Salvage paid $400; Seamen's wages $800; supplying new rigging $900 What per cent. of their goods must each contribute towards the loss? *Ans.* 4 per cent.

15. There are four persons engaged in business as a firm, A, B, C and D. They have been unfortunate, the net loss being $15320. On examination the resources are found to be as follows, viz: Live

Cattle valued at $9680. Packed Beef $12600. Empty Barrels on hand valued at $500. Deposit in Drover's Bank $2500. The firm owe on notes $22600. S. G. Beatty on account $4000. W. B. Robinson on account $6000. The partners invested in equal amounts, and are to share the gains or losses in the same proportion. What was the investment of the firm? What was each partner's investment? *Ans.* Firm $8000. Each partner $2000.

————o————

EXAMINATION No. 3.

————o————

1. A Grocer mixes 50 lbs of Sugar at 10 cts. per lb. with 35 lbs. at 12 cts. and 42 lbs. at 13 cts. What is the mixture worth per lb? *Ans.* .1154 cts.

2. What is the interest on $450 for 1 yr. 11 mo. and 29 days at 9 per cent per annum? *Ans.* 80.8875.

3. Bought 50 gal. Wine at 92 cts. per gal., by accident 10 gal. leaked out. How much must I sell the remainder for in order to gain 10 per cent. on the whole cost? *Ans.* $1.26.

4. What is the capacity in barrels of a circular cistern, 9 feet deep, and 7 feet in diameter? *Ans.* 68.52 barrels.

5. A and B enter into co-partnership, agreeing to share gains and losses according to capital invested. A put in $4000, and B $2540. At the end of 4 months A withdrew $500, and B invested $600. At the end of the year they had gained $3000. How should it be divided? *Ans.* A $1664.99. B $1335.01.

6. There is a conical pile of grain on the floor 12 ft. in diameter and 7 ft. high. How many bushels will be left after filling 2 bins, one 5 ft. 4 in. long, 3 ft. 6 in wide, and 3 ft. deep. The other 5 ft. long, 3 ft. wide and 3 ft. deep? *Ans.* 126.89.

7. My retail price for broadcloth is $4.75 per yd., by which I make a profit of 33⅓ per cent. I sell a wholesale customer 100 yds. at a discount of 30 per cent. from the retail price. What per cent. do I gain or lose, and what do I receive per yard? *Ans.* Lose 6¾ per cent. Received $3.325 per yd.

8. A steamer in her passage from Quebec to Liverpool became stranded when it was found necessary to throw overboard 5000 bbls. of flour belonging to Conger Bros., worth $6.87 per bbl. The expense of getting the vessel off $300, seamen's wages and board $200, supplying new rigging $1500. The vessel was worth $30,000, net freight $3000, goods on board belonging to different merchants amounting to $80000. How much should Conger Bros. receive for their flour. *Ans.* $23452.26.

9. How much will the following lumber cost at $20 per thousand ft. Nine Planks 14 ft. long 1½ in. thick.

Width	17	inches	one end,	19	inches the other.		
"	24	"	"	"	20	"	()	"
"	19	"	"	"	23	"	"	"
"	16	"	"	"	20	"	"	"
"	18	"	"	"	22	"	"	"
"	21	"	"	"	23	"	"	"
"	13	"	"	"	15	"	"	"
"	17	"	"	"	21	"	"	"
"	12	"	"	"	14	"	"	"

Ans. $5.84.

10. What is the compound interest on $1800 for 5 years, at 9 per cent. per annum? *Ans.* $608.806.

11. Holton & Co., in account with James McKay.

Dr.		Cr.	
Jan. 1, to Mdse. $3,000.		April 4, By cash $2,000.	
Mar. 1, "	1,000.	Aug. 15, "	1,000.
May 1, "	2,000.	Nov. 4, "	1,000.

When should a note be dated to balance the above account, all goods being purchased on credit of 3 months? *Ans.* Oct. 31.

12. What is the cost of storage at 3 cts. per barrel per month on flour, received and delivered as follows?

Received.		Delivered.	
June 1, 400 barrels.		Aug. 4, 1,000 barrels.	
" 12, 300 "		" 30, 500 "	
" 26, 100 "		Sep. 1, 500 "	
July 1, 700 "			
" 20, 800 "			

What is the amount of the above account and how many barrels remain on hand Oct. 1st ? *Ans.* 300 bbls. $125.60.

13. I hold a note of $400, dated August 2nd, 1867, bearing interest at 6 per cent., and upon which are the following endorsements : April 2nd, 1868, $50; June 2nd, 1868, $30; January 2nd, 1869, $100. How much remains due March 24th, 1870?
Ans. $269.27.

14. Received from my correspondent in New York $2,000, U. S. Currency, with instructions to deduct my commission at 2½ per cent., and invest the remainder in Canadian Tweeds worth $1.15 per yd. How many yards should I send him? Gold being quoted at $1.14. *Ans.* $1,488.34.

15. Remitted my agent in London, $2,150, Canadian Currency, with instructions to deduct his commission at 2 per cent., and invest the remainder in flour, selling at £1 10s. 6d., sterling. How many barrels should he send? *Ans.* 284 nearly.

————o————

EXAMINATION NO. 4.

1. What is the true discount on a note of $1500 due 60 days hence, discount at 6 per cent. per annum? *Ans.* $14.85.

2. A owes B $1200 payable as follows, $100 in 30 days; $400 in 60 days, and $700 in 90 days. When will the entire debt average due? *Ans.* in 75 days.

3. A and B commence business with a joint capital of $10,000, A is to receive ¾ and B ¼ of the net gain. At the close of the year the resources and liabilities stand as follows :

Resources.		Liabilities.	
Cash,	$8000	Bills payable,	$3000
Merchandise,	7000	Personal Acct. Pay.,	1500
Bills Receiveable,	2000		
Personal Acct. Rec,	1000		

What proportion of the net capital belongs to each partner?

4. What will be the storage of flour at 5 cents per barrel per month, received and delivered as follows : Received 11th of January, 1869, 1300 bbls.; 19th Feby., 700 bbls.; 15th March, 1500. Delivered 29 Jany., 1000 bbls.; 28th Feb., 900 bbls.; 25th March, 1600? *Ans.* $93.66⅔.

5. An insolvent is liable to A for $700, to B for $1000, and to C for $2300. His net worth is $2500. What amount should each creditor receive? *Ans.* A, $437.50; B, $625; C, $1437.50.

6. What is the interest of $1496, for 2 years, 7 months and 18 days, at 6 per cent.? *Ans.* $236.368.

7. A carriage was sold for $500, by which a gain of 20 per cent. was made. What was the cost? *Ans.* $416.66⅔.

8. I own a vessel valued at $7,493, and wish to insure it at a premium of 4⅗ per cent., so as to recover, in case of the destruction of the vessel, both the premium paid and the value of the vessel, for what sum must I insure? *Ans.* $7,854.29.

9. Reduce £749 16s. 5¾d., sterling, to dollars and cents. *Ans.* $3,649.393.

10. Mr. A invested $44,400 in stocks, and sells out for $50,000 What per cent. does he make by the operation? *Ans.* 12.6.

11. A ship in her voyage from New York to Glasgow became stranded, when it was found necessary to throw overboard goods to the amount of $8000. The expense of getting the vessel off was $600; of supplying new rigging $1200. The ship is worth $20,000. Net Freight $2000. Holton & Co. had on board goods worth $16000; Ritchie & Co., goods worth $12000; Conger Bros., goods worth $10,000; Warner Bros., goods worth $2,000. What does each interest contribute towards the loss, and what is the rate per cent. on the contributory interests? *Ans.* Average loss 15⅝ per cent.

12. Receive from my correspondent in New York, $1000, U. S. Currency, with instructions to deduct my commission at 3 per cent., and invest the remainder in Canadian Tweeds, worth $1.25 per yard. How many yards should I send him, gold being quoted at $1.15 ? *Ans.* 675.391.

13. I hold a note of $600, dated January 1st, 1867, bearing interest at 6 per cent., and upon which are the following endorsements :—March 1st, 1868, $200 ; May 1st, 1869, $200. How much is due Jan. 1st, 1870 ? *Ans.* $283.85.

14. A grocer mixes 20 lbs. of sugar at 10c., with 80 lbs. at 12½c., 40 lbs. at 13 c. What is 1 pound of the mixture worth ? *Ans.* 12.28c.

15. I have a conical pile of grain on the floor 12 ft. in diameter and 8 feet high. How much will be left after filling a bin 10 ft. long, 7 ft. 6 inches wide, and 4 feet deep ? *Ans.* 1.24.

www.ingramcontent.com/pod-product-compliance
Lightning Source LLC
Chambersburg PA
CBHW022024190326
41519CB00010B/1595